JONAH/RUTH

Love Crosses Boundaries

A Guided Discovery for Groups and Individuals

Kevin Perrotta

Loyola Press

Chicago

Loyola Press

3441 North Ashland Avenue
Chicago, Illinois 60657

Nihil Obstat
Reverend Charles R. Meyer
Censor Deputatus
April 27, 1999

Imprimatur
Most Reverend Raymond E. Goedert, M.A., S.T.L., J.C.L.
Vicar General
Archdiocese of Chicago
May 7, 1999

The *Nihil Obstat* and *Imprimatur* are official declarations that a book is free of doctrinal and moral error. No implication is contained therein that those who have granted the *Nihil Obstat* and *Imprimatur* agree with the content, opinions, or statements expressed.

The Scripture quotations contained herein are from the New Revised Standard Version Bible: Catholic Edition, copyright © 1993 and 1989 by the Division of Christian Education of the National Council of the Churches of Christ in the U.S.A. Used by permission. All rights reserved. Subheadings in Scripture quotations have been added by the author.

The Latin text of the excerpt from the writings of Nicolaus Serarius can be found in *Iudices et Ruth Explanati* (Moguntinum: Balthasaris Lippii Typographus, 1609). Translation by the author.

Interior design by Kay Hartmann/Communique Design
Illustration by Charise Mericle

ISBN 0-8294-1433-9

Printed in the United States of America
00 01 02 03 04 / 10 9 8 7 6 5 4 3 2 1

Contents

How to Use This Guide

The Bible is like a vast national park filled with various types of terrain and impressive natural features. The park is so big that you could spend months, even years, getting to know it. Is it worth making a brief visit?

In fact, a brief visit to a park, if carefully planned, can be enjoyable and worthwhile. In a few hours you can drive through the park and pull over at a handful of sites. At each stop you can get out of the car, take a short trail through the woods, listen to the wind blowing in the trees, get a feel for the place.

You might compare this booklet to a short visit to a national park. We will read the books of Jonah and Ruth—two of the finest stories in the Bible. Because the stories are quite short, we will be able to take a leisurely walk through each one, thinking carefully about what we are reading and what it means for our lives today. While the books are short, they touch on central themes in God's revelation to us: God's mercy and faithfulness and the response his mercy and faithfulness call forth from us.

This guide provides everything you need to explore Jonah and Ruth in six discussions—or to do a six-part exploration on your own. Introductions (pages 6 and 30) will prepare you to get the most out of your reading. The weekly sections provide explanations that highlight what the words of Scripture mean for us today. Equally important, each section supplies questions that will launch you into fruitful discussion, helping you both to explore Jonah and Ruth for yourself and to learn from one another. If you're using the booklet by yourself, the questions will spur your personal reflection.

Each discussion is meant to be a *guided discovery.*

Guided. None of us is equipped to read the Bible without help. We read the Bible *for* ourselves but not *by* ourselves. Scripture was written to be understood and applied in and with the church. So each week "A Guide to the Reading," drawing on the work of modern biblical scholars and Christian writers of the past, supplies background and explanations. The guide will help you grasp the messages of Jonah and Ruth. Think of it as a friendly park ranger who points out noteworthy details and explains what you're looking at so you can appreciate things for yourself.

Discovery. The purpose is for *you* to interact with God's Word. "Questions for Careful Reading" is a tool to help you dig into Jonah and Ruth and examine them carefully. "Questions for Application" will help you consider what these stories mean for your life here and now. Each week concludes with an "Approach to Prayer" section that helps you respond to God's Word. Supplementary "Living Tradition" and "Saints in the Making" sections offer the thoughts and experiences of Christians past and present in order to show you what Scripture has meant to others—so that you can consider what it might mean for you.

How long are the discussion sessions? We've assumed you will have about an hour and a half when you get together. If you have less time, you'll find that most of the elements can be shortened somewhat.

Is homework necessary? You will get the most out of the discussions if you read the weekly material in advance of each meeting. But if participants are not able to prepare, have someone read the "Guide to the Reading" section aloud to the group at the points where it occurs in the weekly material.

What about leadership? If you happen to have a world-class biblical scholar in your group, by all means ask him or her to lead the discussions. But in the absence of any professional Scripture scholars, or even accomplished biblical amateurs, you can still have a first-class Bible discussion. Choose two or three people to be facilitators, and have everyone read "Suggestions for Bible Discussion Groups" before beginning (page 76).

Does everyone need a guide? a Bible? Everyone in the group will need their own copy of this booklet. It contains the text of Jonah and Ruth, so a Bible is not absolutely necessary—but each participant will find it useful to have one. You should have at least one Bible on hand for your discussion. (See page 80.)

How do we get started? Before you begin, take a look at the suggestions for Bible discussion groups (page 76) and individuals (page 79).

Jonah: A Man Who Was Irritated with God

Centuries before the birth of Christ, an Israelite storyteller asked himself some what-ifs.

What if a genuine prophet refused to cooperate with God, while all around him pagans responded to God at the slightest suggestion?

What if this prophet knew how to compose lovely prayers, but rather than pouring out his inner thoughts to God, he hoarded secret anger against God?

What if he got depressed not because he was unable to get people to turn to the Lord but because he *succeeded* in leading people to turn to the Lord?

Our storyteller stirred these possibilities around, and into his mind came the picture of a prophet: not a Charlton Heston type of prophet, a figure of seriousness and gravity, but a lightweight fellow, a Stan Laurel kind of prophet—the sort of person who, when faced with imminent catastrophe, might take a nap. With this figure in view, the storyteller was ready to put pen to papyrus.

"Now," he began, "the word of the Lord came to Jonah, saying, 'Go at once to Nineveh and cry out against it.' But Jonah set out to flee from the presence of the Lord." The statement "The word of the Lord came to so-and-so" was a standard biblical way of reporting that God had entrusted a message to a prophet. "So-and-so set out to flee from the presence of the Lord" was a very nonstandard way for a prophet to respond! Obviously Jonah was going to be an unusual prophet.

Reading the story of Jonah, we can sense that the author was pleased with his literary creation. Jonah is an entertaining non-hero. We have no way of knowing whether the author also thought that his story was inspired by God. But many people in Israel did. They recognized in this little story a message from God, and they showed their recognition by placing it in the library of Israel's inspired writings—the library that has become the Old Testament of the Christian Bible.

In the library of the Bible we find history and law, prophecies and letters. Amid these imposing volumes, is there a place for a little humor? Apparently so, for if humor lies in perceiving an incongruity, there is plenty of humor in this short story. At every turn, Jonah violates the expectations that Israelite readers would have had. For example, Abraham prayed for the wicked city of Sodom to be spared divine retribution; Jonah gets angry because God *does* spare a city. Job cried out in anger against the Lord for being harsh to the innocent; Jonah cries out in protest because the Lord shows mercy to the guilty. Elsewhere in the Bible, the people of Israel often reject the warnings of prophets, even when they speak at length. In the book of Jonah, pagans respond as soon as a prophet opens his mouth.

Of course, to describe the story of Jonah as humorous is not to say that it is not also serious. Everyone who has ever laughed at a political cartoon knows how serious humor can be.

Detecting the serious issues beneath the surface of the story is part of the enjoyment of reading Jonah. I will not spoil the fun by offering a full-scale discussion in this introduction. Before we begin, however, it may be helpful to explain a few elements in the story's background. This background was familiar to the ancient audience but is unfamiliar to most of us today.

The author identifies the Jonah of the story with a real Jonah, Jonah son of Amittai, who lived in the eighth century before Christ and is briefly mentioned in one of the historical books of the Bible (2 Kings 14:25). This places Jonah at a particular point in Israel's history: the story takes place a generation or so before the armies of the Assyrian Empire descended on Israel, grinding the northern portion of the country to dust and turning the southern portion into a political satellite.

Even in an age of ruthless warfare, the Assyrians were known for their savagery. They incinerated cities, drove people from their homes, and abused prisoners of war. One of the Assyrian emperor's palaces was decorated with wall panels that proudly showed his soldiers performing what today we would call military atrocities and crimes against humanity.

It is to the capital of this evil empire, to Nineveh (in present-day Iraq), that God sends Jonah to preach. The first readers of the story lived after the Assyrian onslaught. They could readily understand why Jonah might have been reluctant to carry out such a mission.

I have spoken of Jonah as a short story. Did it not really happen? Some readers may wonder whether denying that Jonah is historical betrays skepticism about miracles, with which the story is loaded. Does interpreting Jonah as fiction reduce its importance?

For centuries Christians and Jews did consider the story of Jonah to be historical. In the fifth century, for example, Cyril, the bishop of Alexandria in Egypt, defended the story against the charge that the miracles it recounts are impossible. "Certainly what happened to Jonah is unexpected and beyond reason and custom," Cyril admitted. "But if the all-powerful God wished to accomplish it, who will refuse to believe it?" Cyril refuted the arguments of the book's pagan mockers by pointing out that in their own religious literature they encountered many things stranger than a sea monster saving a prophet by swallowing him.

However, it is not because of skepticism but because of an analysis of the text itself, its language and style, that most scholars today regard Jonah as an imaginative story. And this view does not make the story less important, any more than Jesus' stories about a kindly Samaritan and a wayward son (Luke 10; 15) are less important than accounts of actual people. The questions the book of Jonah raises are no less serious and the messages it conveys are no less true than if the story were historical fact.

Before you begin to read the book of Jonah, let me offer a few suggestions for how to get the most out of your reading:

✦ The author refrained from telling us everything we might like to know about why Jonah does what he does; this forces us to try to figure Jonah out for ourselves. Jonah is a puzzling person, so be prepared to be puzzled! Be ready for a story where the storyteller leaves us guessing until the end—and even then.

✦ The author of Jonah was a talented storyteller (it seems a shame that none of his other stories have survived). The story is very cleverly put together. Every word counts. To get the most out of the story, slow down! Read carefully, and reread. I suggest reading the whole story in one sitting. It doesn't take long. (The text is given in Weeks 1 and 2.)

+ As you read, ask yourself, How am I like Jonah—and do I want to be? At the end of the story, God puts a question to Jonah that challenges him to change. In what way is God's question also directed to you? What would it mean for you to answer God's question?

+ When you get to the end, ask yourself, What is the central, serious issue that underlies this story? Why did the author decide to deal with this issue by means of a little humor? What makes this issue so difficult to confront? Where do I face this issue in my own life?

FLIGHT, STORM, AND RESCUE

Questions to Begin

15 minutes
Use a question or two to get warmed up for the reading.

1 What was your scariest experience while traveling?

2 When has a stranger been especially helpful to you on a trip?

3 Describe an incident when danger spurred you to pray.

Opening the Bible

5 minutes
Read the passage aloud. Let individuals take turns reading
paragraphs.

The Reading: Jonah 1:1–2:10

"This Is a Fine Mess You've Gotten Us Into!"

1 Now the word of the LORD came to Jonah son of Amittai, saying,
2 "Go at once to Nineveh, that great city, and cry out against it; for
their wickedness has come up before me." 3 But Jonah set out to flee
to Tarshish from the presence of the LORD. He went down to Joppa
and found a ship going to Tarshish; so he paid his fare and went on
board, to go with them to Tarshish, away from the presence of the
LORD. 4 But the LORD hurled a great wind upon the sea, and such
a mighty storm came upon the sea that the ship threatened to break
up. 5 Then the mariners were afraid, and each cried to his god. They
threw the cargo that was in the ship into the sea, to lighten it for them.
Jonah, meanwhile, had gone down into the hold of the ship and had
lain down, and was fast asleep. 6 The captain came and said to him,
"What are you doing sound asleep? Get up, call on your god! Perhaps
the god will spare us a thought so that we do not perish."

7 The sailors said to one another, "Come, let us cast lots,
so that we may know on whose account this calamity has come upon
us." So they cast lots, and the lot fell on Jonah. 8 Then they said to
him, "Tell us why this calamity has come upon us. What is your occupation? Where do you come from? What is your country? And of
what people are you?"

9 "I am a Hebrew," he replied. "I worship the LORD, the
God of heaven, who made the sea and the dry land."

10 Then the men were even more afraid, and said to him,
"What is this that you have done!" For the men knew that he was
fleeing from the presence of the LORD, because he had told them
so. 11 Then they said to him, "What shall we do to you, that the sea
may quiet down for us?" For the sea was growing more and more
tempestuous.

12 He said to them, "Pick me up and throw me into the sea;
then the sea will quiet down for you; for I know it is because of me
that this great storm has come upon you."

13 Nevertheless the men rowed hard to bring the ship back
to land, but they could not, for the sea grew more and more stormy
against them. 14 Then they cried out to the LORD, "Please, O LORD,

we pray, do not let us perish on account of this man's life. Do not make us guilty of innocent blood; for you, O LORD, have done as it pleased you." 15 So they picked Jonah up and threw him into the sea; and the sea ceased from its raging. 16 Then the men feared the LORD even more, and they offered a sacrifice to the LORD and made vows.

17 But the LORD provided a large fish to swallow up Jonah; and Jonah was in the belly of the fish three days and three nights.

A Prayer in an Unusual Location

2:1 Then Jonah prayed to the LORD his God from the belly of the fish, 2 saying,

> "I called to the LORD out of my distress,
>   and he answered me;
> out of the belly of Sheol I cried,
>   and you heard my voice.
> 3 You cast me into the deep,
>   into the heart of the seas . . .
>   all your waves and your billows
>   passed over me. . . .
> 5 The waters closed in over me;
>   the deep surrounded me;
>   weeds were wrapped around my head
> 6   at the roots of the mountains.
>   I went down to the land
>   whose bars closed upon me forever;
>   yet you brought up my life from the Pit,
>   O LORD my God. . . .
> 9 But I with the voice of thanksgiving
>   will sacrifice to you;
>   what I have vowed I will pay.
>   Deliverance belongs to the LORD!"

10 Then the LORD spoke to the fish, and it spewed Jonah out upon the dry land.

Questions for Careful Reading

10 minutes
Choose questions according to your interest and time.

1 What are the sailors afraid of in 1:5, 10, and 16?

2 What differences are there between Jonah and the sailors? Who knows more about God? What does it mean to know God? Who is closer to God— Jonah or the sailors? In what way?

3 In his prayer Jonah says he called to the Lord out of his distress (2:2). Does he show an awareness of how he got into distress? Jonah says to God, "You cast me into the deep" (2:3). Does Jonah acknowledge his own responsibility for what has happened?

4 What picture of God emerges from this reading?

A Guide to the Reading

If participants have not read this section already, read it aloud. Otherwise go on to "Questions for Application."

1:1–3. The author gives us the gist of the message God assigns to Jonah: "cry out against" Nineveh means "proclaim doom" on it. We are left guessing why Jonah does not welcome the opportunity to deliver this message against his country's brutal enemy. Whatever Jonah's reason, it must be serious, because he books passage for Tarshish. Scholars disagree about exactly where Tarshish was, but they do agree it was far (think buying a one-way ticket to Uzbekistan).

1:4–6. When a storm strikes, the sailors turn out to be pious men. They pray first, take action second. Jonah does neither but goes down into the hold and falls asleep (whether before or during the storm is unclear). Commentators through the centuries have wrestled with this puzzling behavior. St. Jerome, a fourth-century biblical scholar, suggested that either Jonah was blithely unaware of the danger his sin had brought on him (like many of us) or, aware of his sin, Jonah went below to escape the sight of the waves, which he understood as a message of divine anger. But if he was scared, how did he fall asleep? In any case, when the captain finds Jonah snoozing, he does not ask his help, just his prayers. But we do not hear that Jonah complied with his request.

1:7–12. The sailors guess that a god must be angry with someone on board, and they cast lots to find out who it is. When the lot falls to Jonah, they do not immediately toss him overboard but give him a chance to explain himself. Jonah boasts that his God is the creator of the sea and the dry land—which is true, but sounds odd coming from Jonah, who has done his best to get away from this God. And if Jonah believed God made the sea, why did he take an ocean voyage to escape him?

Jonah's advice to throw him overboard seems self-sacrificing. Yet he certainly waited long enough before suggesting it! In view of his failure to pray, one commentator suggests that Jonah preferred to die rather than to seek the help of the God he was fleeing.

1:13–16. The sailors are afraid of angering God by drowning Jonah. So they row toward the coast in order to release him on dry land—a desperate move, because bringing the ship near land increases the danger of shipwreck. (If you had to choose a crew, these considerate guys would be the ones to sail with.) Their effort fails, so, afraid for their lives, they say a quick prayer and give Jonah the heave-ho. The sudden calm frightens them even more than the storm, and they offer sacrifices to Jonah's God. One commentator remarks, "Jonah's very rebelliousness can be turned to serve God's purpose!"

In chapter 1. Notice that the action begins with "the word of the Lord." God's word turns out to be powerful and persistent. When Jonah runs away, God's words and actions pursue him. For example, God *hurls* a wind on the sea (1:4); the sailors *throw* the cargo into the sea (1:5); then they *throw* Jonah into the sea (1:15). The same Hebrew word is used each time—and then disappears from the story. It is as though God's words and acts, once released into the world, continue to echo until they achieve their purpose. At the beginning the Lord told Jonah to "cry out" against Nineveh. This same Hebrew word has already echoed in verses 5, 6, and 14, and it will continue to echo until it too reaches fulfillment.

2:1–9. Whatever Jonah's earlier reluctance to talk to God, he starts praying as soon as he hits the water. We do not hear this prayer for help, but when Jonah thanks God for rescuing him, he recalls that he "cried" to the Lord (verse 2—that same Hebrew "cry out" word continuing to echo). God's way of rescuing Jonah from drowning, by means of a giant fish, is unusual, but Jonah is an unusual prophet. Does God deal differently with different people? After sitting inside the fish for three days, Jonah thanks God for saving him. Why did it take Jonah so long?

Jonah's prayer is like many prayers in the book of Psalms, and its standardized quality does not allow us to see what Jonah personally thinks. Clearly he knows how to offer a nice thanksgiving prayer. But does he recognize he was wrong to run away from the mission God gave him? Is Jonah telling God everything that is on his mind?

Questions for Application

40 minutes
Choose questions according to your interest and time.

1 How are you like Jonah?

2 When have you tried to escape from what God wanted you to do—perhaps from a change God wanted you to make in your life or from a responsibility to another person? In what ways did God pursue you and continue to insist on his will for you? Did God catch up with you?

3 When you try to run away from God, what is the "Tarshish" you head toward? the ship you sail on? Is it watching TV, shopping, working? Where does your mind escape to when it is time to pray?

4 Where do you see contradictions between what you believe about God and how you relate to him?

5 Are you sometimes reluctant to pray? Why?

6 Are you good at saying the "right" things—the things people expect? Is this a help or a hindrance? When you pray, do you sometimes say the "right" things to God without being completely honest about what you are thinking and feeling?

"Look for the main theme within the passage before you start analyzing its constituent parts."

Christine Dodd, *Making Scripture Work*

Approach to Prayer

15 minutes
Use one of these approaches—or create your own!

✦ Invite participants to briefly mention a situation in which God has rescued them from danger or sin. Then pray Jonah's psalm together as an expression of thanks to God.

✦ Invite participants to briefly mention an area of life in which they feel they need to listen more carefully for God's guidance or need to respond more readily to God's will. Then pray Psalm 81 together.

A Living Tradition

Jonah as an Image of Christ

This section is a supplement for individual reading.

When the early Christians read the Bible, they delighted to discover ways that figures in Israel's history foreshadowed Jesus. For example, St. Cyril of Alexandria, who lived in Egypt in the fifth century, found parallels between Jonah and Jesus. Jonah was in a fish for three days and was then restored to land. This made him an image of Jesus, who lay in the earth three days and rose to new life.

Of course, Cyril acknowledged, not everything about Jonah was Christlike. Jonah was sorry to see the Ninevites repenting, while Jesus is never displeased when anyone turns from sin. Cyril remarked, "Jonah provides images of the mystery of Christ. But one would not for that reason think that everything that happened to him was useful for spiritual contemplation."

Cyril saw a striking parallel between the calming of the storm by Jonah's being thrown overboard and the salvation of the world by Christ. Before Christ came, Cyril wrote, the whole world was in danger: The human race was like a ship driven by storms, "the waves of sin were all but rushing down on it, dangerous and irresistible cravings for pleasure washing all around, wave after wave of destruction rising up against it, and fierce winds—the winds of the devil and his evil forces with him—were breaking upon it.

"But when we were in such a state of things, the creator had mercy. God the Father sent his Son to us from heaven. He came in human flesh, and having arrived on the endangered and storm-tossed earth, he gave himself willingly to death in order to halt the waves, to calm the sea, to lull the billows. We have been saved by the death of Christ! The storm has driven past, the ocean swells have been smoothed, the force of the winds has abated. From now on, a deep stillness spreads over the sea, and we have tranquillity in our thoughts, now that Christ has suffered on our account."

ANGERED BY LOVE

Questions to Begin

15 minutes
Use a question or two to get warmed up for the reading.

1 What duties do you typically need to be reminded to do? If you're married, how would your spouse answer this question?

2 What little problems have the potential to make you unreasonably angry?

3 If you could choose any plant in the world, what plant would you wish to own?

5 minutes
Read the passage aloud. Let individuals take turns reading
paragraphs.

The Reading: Jonah 3:1–4:11

A Powerfully Effective Prophetic Word

1 The word of the LORD came to Jonah a second time, saying, 2 "Get up, go to Nineveh, that great city, and proclaim to it the message that I tell you." 3 So Jonah set out and went to Nineveh, according to the word of the LORD. Now Nineveh was an exceedingly large city, a three days' walk across.

4 Jonah began to go into the city, going a day's walk. And he cried out, "Forty days more, and Nineveh shall be overthrown!" 5 And the people of Nineveh believed God; they proclaimed a fast, and everyone, great and small, put on sackcloth.

6 When the news reached the king of Nineveh, he rose from his throne, removed his robe, covered himself with sackcloth, and sat in ashes. 7 Then he had a proclamation made in Nineveh: "By the decree of the king and his nobles: No human being or animal, no herd or flock, shall taste anything. They shall not feed, nor shall they drink water. 8 Human beings and animals shall be covered with sackcloth, and they shall cry mightily to God. All shall turn from their evil ways and from the violence that is in their hands. 9 Who knows? God may relent and change his mind; he may turn from his fierce anger, so that we do not perish."

10 When God saw what they did, how they turned from their evil ways, God changed his mind about the calamity that he had said he would bring upon them; and he did not do it.

More Effective Than the Prophet Wanted

4:1 But this was very displeasing to Jonah, and he became angry. 2 He prayed to the LORD and said, "O LORD! Is not this what I said while I was still in my own country? That is why I fled to Tarshish at the beginning; for I knew that you are a gracious God and merciful, slow to anger, and abounding in steadfast love, and ready to relent from punishing. 3 And now, O LORD, please take my life from me, for it is better for me to die than to live."

4 And the LORD said, "Is it right for you to be angry?"

⁵ Then Jonah went out of the city and sat down east of the city, and made a booth for himself there. He sat under it in the shade, waiting to see what would become of the city.

⁶ The Lord God appointed a bush, and made it come up over Jonah, to give shade over his head, to save him from his discomfort; so Jonah was very happy about the bush. ⁷ But when dawn came up the next day, God appointed a worm that attacked the bush, so that it withered. ⁸ When the sun rose, God prepared a sultry east wind, and the sun beat down on the head of Jonah so that he was faint and asked that he might die. He said, "It is better for me to die than to live."

⁹ But God said to Jonah, "Is it right for you to be angry about the bush?"

And he said, "Yes, angry enough to die."

¹⁰ Then the Lord said, "You are concerned about the bush, for which you did not labor and which you did not grow; it came into being in a night and perished in a night. ¹¹ And should I not be concerned about Nineveh, that great city, in which there are more than a hundred and twenty thousand persons who do not know their right hand from their left, and also many animals?"

10 minutes
Choose questions according to your interest and time.

1   What does Jonah seem to know about God and about what God is going to do? What does he seem not to know?

2   Among the Ninevites' various actions, which does God respond to?

3   How does Jonah's response to God compare with the Ninevites' response to God?

4   Judging from 4:1–3, is Jonah sorry for having refused to carry out the mission God gave him?

5   Compare Jonah's prayers in 2:2–9 and 4:1–3. How well do they fit together?

6   How do chapters 3 and 4 deepen the portrait of God reflected in chapters 1 and 2? In what way does God change in the story? In what way does he not change?

A Guide to the Reading

*If participants have not read this section already, read it aloud.
Otherwise go on to "Questions for Application."*

3:1. Why did God repeat his instructions to Jonah? Perhaps Jonah was planning to go back to Jerusalem to offer thanks for his rescue (2:9), hoping God had forgotten about the Nineveh mission. Biblical scholar Jonathan Magonet remarks that "for Jonah the re-treat into piety is yet another evasion of the call from God—when flight from God did not work, there is always a flight to God, or to that convenient God who makes no demands beyond those the worshipper can comfortably offer."

3:4. Finally Jonah cries out as he was told to do. His message is bleak. But, St. Jerome argues, it shows that God would rather forgive than destroy, since "no one who wants to punish is-sues beforehand a warning of what they are going to do." God's forty-day notice to the Ninevites implicitly invites them to repent.

3:5–8. The king directs his people to "cry mightily to God" (3:8). With this cry of repentance, God's original command to Jonah to cry out has now achieved its purpose, and the word *cry* is not used again in the story.

4:1–4. God's words to Jonah in verse 4 could be trans-lated, "You really *are* angry!" What causes Jonah's rage? The fol-lowing are possible reasons for his anger:

+ He doesn't want to see an enemy of his people go unpunished.

+ He doesn't want God to extend to other nations the mercy he has shown to Israel.

+ He is a champion of rigid justice, offended by God's softness toward evildoers.

+ He feels embarrassed because what he predicted has not occurred.

Perhaps, as in a multiple-choice test, there is another pos-sibility: all of the above. Earlier we wondered why, in his prayer in the fish, Jonah failed to express repentance for fleeing from God. His prayer now answers the question. Jonah never stopped thinking that his God-given mission to Nineveh was a bad idea. Jonah knew it would provide the Ninevites with the opportunity to repent and find mercy—and that was an opportunity Jonah did not want the Ninevites to have.

Jonah's clash of wills with God, suppressed in chapter 1, now breaks into the open. Jonah stands face-to-face with God. "Is not this what I said while I was still in my own country? That is why I fled to Tarshish at the beginning; for I knew . . ." (4:2).

Jonah declares that he knows God—and it is true. In contrast to the pagan mariners and city dwellers, who have only dim ideas of God's justice and mercy (1:6; 3:9), Jonah the Israelite knows God (1:9; 4:2). Yet what he knows about God does not please him. He does not like a God who is patient and prefers not to punish. Yet where would Jonah be if God had not been merciful and lenient during the storm at sea?

4:5. Just as Jonah refused to pray on the boat, now he refuses to answer God's question. Jonah knows that God has forgiven the Ninevites, yet he goes out of the city to see what will happen. How much sense does that make? Earlier he fled from God by ship, knowing that God created the sea. Do Jonah's desires blind him to the realities he already knows?

4:8. Jonah is as angry at the withering of the bush as he was at the sparing of Nineveh (4:1). That suggests he would have found the city's destruction as enjoyable as the bush's refreshing shade on a scorchingly hot day.

4:10–11. God does not belittle Jonah's anger over the plant's demise. A person exposed to sun and hot winds is understandably sorry to have his shade taken away. Rather God takes issue with Jonah's anger at God's mercy toward Nineveh. God draws a parallel: just as Jonah was happy to have a big, leafy bush to shade him on a hot day, so God was happy to have a big city full of people, even if they were guilty of violence and injustice! God hates violence, but he likes his creatures. They make him happy. Can't Jonah bring himself to share in that happiness?

God's question will continue to hang in the air until it achieves its purpose in Jonah—and in us. Will we share in God's fondness for our fellow human beings, imperfect as they are?

Questions for Application

40 minutes
Choose questions according to your interest and time.

1 What pious practices would you rather substitute for obedience to the tasks that God has set before you?

2 Have you ever felt that God has let you down? What happened?

3 Whom do you find it difficult to forgive? Do deathbed conversions bother you? What might God be saying to you about this attitude through the book of Jonah?

4 The book of Jonah suggests that people without any religious commitment can be more responsive to God than people who are religious. What are your observations about this suggestion? What implications does it have for you?

5 When is it appropriate to warn people about the consequences of their behavior? Think of your experience in giving people warnings. Have the results (good or bad) sometimes been unexpected? How have you responded to warnings?

"Are you able to admit that you do not have all the answers about the Bible? God? Your own life?"

Serendipity House group Bible study, *1 John/Galatians*

Approach to Prayer

15 minutes
Use this approach—or create your own!

✦ Allow participants to think of those whom they find it difficult to forgive. Then let someone read aloud Luke 6:27–36. Pause for a few minutes of silence, and end by praying the Our Father together.

Saints in the Making

The Grace to Forgive

This section is a supplement for individual reading.

Corrie ten Boom was a middle-aged watchmaker in Haarlem, Holland, living quietly with her father, Casper, and her older sister, Betsy, when Germany invaded the Netherlands in 1941. The German occupation was brutal, but if the ten Booms had lain low, they would probably have been able to stay out of harm's way. However, when the Germans began to round up Jewish citizens and transport them to extermination camps, the ten Booms opened their home to several Jews. Using a hiding place in the attic of their narrow, old town house, the ten Booms, who were Christians, succeeded in concealing Jewish friends from German authorities. But the trio was caught violating the food-rationing law.

Elderly Casper ten Boom died within weeks of his arrest. The sisters were shipped to the German concentration camp in Ravensbrück. There, after months of suffering, Betsy died. Corrie, slated for the gas chamber, was unexpectedly released as the result of a clerical error.

After the war Corrie traveled in Germany, speaking about her experience of God's faithfulness amid suffering. In her book *The Hiding Place* she described meeting a man who had been a guard at Ravensbrück. He had since become a Christian, and he came up after her talk to thank her for her message. As he extended his hand to greet her, Corrie wrote, "the roomful of mocking men, the heaps of clothing, Betsy's pain-blanched face" flashed in her mind. Despite her preaching about forgiveness, her hand hung at her side.

"Even as angry, vengeful thoughts boiled over me," she wrote, "I saw the sin of them." But she was unable to forgive. "I felt not the slightest spark of warmth or charity." After an inner struggle, however, she prayed, "Jesus, I cannot forgive him. Give me Your forgiveness." Only then did she feel able to grasp the hand of her former tormentor. "As I took his hand," she wrote, "into my heart sprang a love for this stranger that almost overwhelmed me."

With God's grace, Corrie did what Jonah refused to do: she welcomed the repentance of an enemy.

Ruth: A Woman Who Showed God's Faithfulness

If you have ever lived in a foreign country, if you have been deeply grieved by the death of a loved one, or if hardships have ever brought you to a point of hopelessness and anger at God, you will probably appreciate the book of Ruth. It tells about two women who suffer bereavement and poverty—an Israelite named Naomi and her foreign daughter-in-law Ruth.

The book of Ruth shows how God uses human faithfulness and generosity to restore life, but it also honestly portrays the pain that great losses can inflict on us. Its first scene is filled with tears, and tears are also a good starting point for reading Ruth. The author uses a minimum of detail to tell of Naomi's and Ruth's difficulties. He expects us to fill in the gaps from our own experience of dislocation and grief.

Considering how short the book of Ruth is, it comprises a surprisingly wide range of situations. Courtship and marriage, birth and death, hunger and aging, family obligations and inheritance— all these human universals enter into four brief chapters. The common human quality of these experiences makes the story easy for all of us to relate to, no matter what our own background and circumstances may be.

These universals take a particular shape in each culture, however. Marriage and family life looked somewhat different in ancient Bethlehem, where the story is set, from the way they look in, say, modern Boston. Opening the book of Ruth, we enter a foreign culture. Until we learn a little about life in Bethlehem some three thousand years ago, certain points will remain puzzling. Why does Naomi tell her daughters-in-law to leave her because she is unable to have any more children? Why is there a question about who has first dibs on marrying Ruth? To shed light on such matters, the guides to the reading will offer some information about the cultural background of the story.

Before we begin, it is useful to know something of the story's historical setting. The action moves back and forth between Judah and Moab. Judah is the region south of Jerusalem and west of the Dead Sea, an area divided today between Israeli and Palestinian rule. Moab is east of the Dead Sea, in modern Jordan.

At the beginning of the story Naomi and her family leave Bethlehem, in Judah, and travel to Moab, a few days' journey away (1:1). Later Naomi returns (1:19). The story takes place more than a thousand years before Christ, in the period before there were kings in Israel —some three centuries before the story of Jonah. Regional strongmen called judges provided leadership (1:1).

The book of Ruth is a time-out from the march of major events in the history of Israel. In Ruth no kings rise or fall, no battles are fought, no cities are plundered, and no temple is constructed. The story involves ordinary people in ordinary situations. Yet Israel's history and the book of Ruth are not disconnected. In fact, they are tied together in several ways.

Elsewhere in the Bible we see the great theme of God's faithfulness to his people being played out on the level of royal court and national temple. In Ruth we see God's faithfulness on the level of clan and village. The author shows God expressing his faithfulness to his people not by steering national and international events but by shaping the circumstances of individuals who embody his kindness.

At the end of the story we learn that the main characters are ancestors of the kings of Israel. Thus we see that the private decisions of individuals are interwoven with the development of God's people. On the one hand, the welfare of the nation as a whole depends on the uprightness and generosity of individual members and their family bonds. John Paul II's remark "History is passing by way of the family" comes to mind; in other words, larger events are shaped by the kinds of people our families produce. On the other hand, individuals find their fulfillment in contributing to the common good of God's people.

A final bit of advice. Although Ruth is twice as long as Jonah, it is still quite short. Try reading it in one sitting in order to get the whole story. Then reread it slowly as you prepare for each discussion.

Three Widows

Questions to Begin

15 minutes
Use a question or two to get warmed up for the reading.

1 What family member do you especially admire for his or her loyalty to others?

2 Why might a mother-in-law and a daughter-in-law not get along? What does a healthy mother-in-law–daughter-in-law relationship look like? Do mothers-in-law suffer from unfair stereotyping?

3 What piece of music do you associate with grief or loss?

4 How has commitment to another person taken you on a journey into the unknown?

5 minutes
Read the passage aloud. Let individuals take turns reading
paragraphs.

The Reading: Ruth 1:1–22

A Series of Losses

[1] In the days when the judges ruled, there was a famine in the land, and a certain man of Bethlehem in Judah went to live in the country of Moab, he and his wife and two sons. [2] The name of the man was Elimelech and the name of his wife Naomi, and the names of his two sons were Mahlon and Chilion; they were Ephrathites from Bethlehem in Judah. They went into the country of Moab and remained there. [3] But Elimelech, the husband of Naomi, died, and she was left with her two sons. [4] These took Moabite wives; the name of the one was Orpah and the name of the other Ruth. When they had lived there about ten years, [5] both Mahlon and Chilion also died, so that the woman was left without her two sons and her husband.

Going Back Home

[6] Then she started to return with her daughters-in-law from the country of Moab, for she had heard in the country of Moab that the LORD had considered his people and given them food. [7] So she set out from the place where she had been living, she and her two daughters-in-law, and they went on their way to go back to the land of Judah. [8] But Naomi said to her two daughters-in-law, "Go back each of you to your mother's house. May the LORD deal kindly with you, as you have dealt with the dead and with me. [9] The LORD grant that you may find security, each of you in the house of your husband." Then she kissed them, and they wept aloud. [10] They said to her, "No, we will return with you to your people."

[11] But Naomi said, "Turn back, my daughters, why will you go with me? Do I still have sons in my womb that they may become your husbands? [12] Turn back, my daughters, go your way, for I am too old to have a husband. Even if I thought there was hope for me, even if I should have a husband tonight and bear sons, [13] would you then wait until they were grown? Would you then refrain from marrying? No, my daughters, it has been far more bitter for me than for you, because the hand of the LORD has turned against me." [14] Then they wept aloud again. Orpah kissed her mother-in-law, but Ruth clung to her.

^{15} So she said, "See, your sister-in-law has gone back to her people and to her gods; return after your sister-in-law." ^{16} But Ruth said,

> "Do not press me to leave you
>> or to turn back from following you!
> Where you go, I will go;
>> Where you lodge, I will lodge;
> your people shall be my people,
>> and your God my God.
> ^{17} Where you die, I will die—
>> there will I be buried.
> May the LORD do thus and so to me,
>> and more as well,
> if even death parts me from you!"

^{18} When Naomi saw that she was determined to go with her, she said no more to her.

Empty and Bitter

^{19} So the two of them went on until they came to Bethlehem. When they came to Bethlehem, the whole town was stirred because of them; and the women said, "Is this Naomi?" ^{20} She said to them,

> "Call me no longer Naomi,
>> call me Mara,
>> for the Almighty has dealt bitterly with me.
> ^{21} I went away full,
>> but the LORD has brought me back empty;
> why call me Naomi
>> when the LORD has dealt harshly with me,
>> and the Almighty has brought calamity upon me?"

^{22} So Naomi returned together with Ruth the Moabite, her daughter-in-law, who came back with her from the country of Moab. They came to Bethlehem at the beginning of the barley harvest.

Questions for Careful Reading

10 minutes
Choose questions according to your interest and time.

1 Does the author seem to think Orpah is wrong to leave Naomi? Do you?

2 How would you characterize Naomi's relationship with God (see 1:6, 8, 20, 21)?

3 What response does Naomi make to Ruth's profession of loyalty (1:16–17)? How does Naomi relate to Ruth in the remainder of chapter 1?

4 In verse 21 Naomi says, "The LORD has brought me back empty." Is Naomi completely empty?

5 At the end of chapter 1, what are the problems to be solved and the questions to be answered in this story?

A Guide to the Reading

If participants have not read this section already, read it aloud. Otherwise go on to "Questions for Application."

1:1–5. The author covers Naomi's decade of misfortune in a few stark sentences, trusting that we will be able to imagine the details of her grief. The ancient audience would sense not only her sorrow but also her peril. Without husband, sons, or grandsons, what will become of her? Naomi may be only in her forties, but her life seems to be over.

1:6–13. Naomi's abandonments have come in stages. The final separation—from her daughters-in-law—she must initiate herself. Only on the road to Judah does Naomi send them away (1:7–14). Did she dread the parting?

All three women face the reality that, in their peasant culture, a woman needs to be part of a household headed by a man. What household will these widows belong to now? If Mahlon and Chilion had had brothers, they would normally have married their deceased brothers' widows—even if they themselves were already married. A man could have more than one wife, and marrying his brother's widow was a way of providing for her. But Mahlon and Chilion did not and are not going to have any brothers. So it would be natural for the daughters-in-law to return to their families, who may be able to arrange for them to marry again.

1:14–17. Orpah is persuaded to go back, but Ruth refuses to leave Naomi. "Where you lodge, I will lodge," Ruth declares (1:16), using a word that means "spend the night" (modern Hebrew constructs its word for hotel from this word). Ruth is committing herself to share the uncertainty of Naomi's life. She will accompany Naomi both in life and in death: ultimately their bones will rest together in the same family burial pit (1:17).

Ruth's decision to leave family and country strikes a note heard in the story of Abraham. God also called Abraham (then known as Abram) to travel to a foreign country. In fact, Ruth is setting out for the same land that God called Abraham to. God gave Abraham an explicit summons to leave home; in contrast, Ruth does not receive a message from God. Yet God's call comes to Ruth all the same: Naomi in need is God's unspoken invitation to Ruth to leave family and country and set out into the unknown.

Ruth is not an Israelite but belongs to the neighboring Moabite people. The Moabites have their own gods. But in her vow to Naomi, Ruth professes loyalty to Naomi's God, the God of Israel (1:16). Only here does Ruth speak the name of Israel's God—"the LORD" (1:17). It is her faithfulness to her mother-in-law that brings her into relationship with God. She responds to God's grace in the form in which it presents itself: the opportunity to serve a needy relative.

Ruth shows Naomi a loyalty that could be described by a Hebrew word meaning "generous faithfulness in need" (*hesed*—translated "deal kindly," 1:8; "kindness," 2:20; "loyalty," 3:10). She shows her faithfulness, inasmuch as she already has a relationship with Naomi. With Naomi in unusual need, Ruth undertakes to care for her in a way that goes beyond what is expected. While the story is named after Ruth, the central actor, it could also be entitled "Generous Faithfulness in Need."

1:18–22. It might also be called "Naomi," for Naomi's emptiness is the central problem to be solved. And the first chapter shows us not only Naomi's situation but also her reactions to it. Commentator Frederic Bush observes that Naomi's rhetorical questions in verses 11 through 13 are not part of a logical argument. "She is not really giving reasons at all. Rather, this is the anguished, almost angry, cry of a woman overwhelmed by the bitter knowledge that she must return home alone and cannot drag two young women into the hopelessness of her widowed and lonely state." Arriving in Bethlehem, she cuts off the women's delighted welcome with a depressed response: "Don't call me Naomi"— which means "delightful," "pleasant," "sweet." "Call me Mara"—which means "bitter."

As an Israelite who believes that everything is under God's authority, Naomi holds God personally responsible for her pain. Her words bear a note of complaint against God. The God of Israel— the God of covenant faithfulness—has let Naomi and her family suffer. Has God been unfair to Naomi? Has he abandoned her? Hold on to those questions!

Questions for Application

40 minutes
Choose questions according to your interest and time.

1 Do hardships make it difficult for you to recognize the blessings you have? Can hardship make you bitter? When have you suffered losses that made it difficult to have any hope? How did you come through it?

2 When serious losses drain a person's hope, what is the best way to help?

3 If Naomi lived in your parish, would you know about her situation? What kind of support would she receive?

4 Is there a Naomi—a particularly needy person, female or male—among your relatives? in your neighborhood? What kind of care does this person need? What are their unmet needs? How can you contribute?

5 When have you faced a choice about caring for someone who was very needy? What did you do? How did things turn out?

6 When you feel disappointed or angry with God, do you express your feelings to him honestly? Is this dangerous to do? healthy? Why?

"For the sessions to be fruitful, you need to spend time in prayerful reflection on the passage to be discussed."

John Burke, O.P., *Beginners' Guide to Bible Sharing*

Approach to Prayer

15 minutes
Use this approach—or create your own!

✦ Let someone in the group
read aloud James 1:22–27
and 2:14–17, and allow a few
minutes for silent reflection.
Give participants an opportunity to pray brief prayers aloud
for people they know who are
suffering from a loss or a serious
need of some sort. The leader
can sum up the prayers with
a final prayer asking God to
guide each person in the group
in expressing care for those
who have been mentioned.
End by praying the Our Father
together.

Saints in the Making

Where You Grow Old, There I Will Grow Old

This section is a supplement for individual reading.

My aunt Ursula was almost the oldest of ten children, my uncle Eric almost the youngest. Paradoxically the fifteen years that lay between them brought them together, for the difference in age put Ursula in the position to be a second mother to her younger brother.

Neither Ursula nor Eric married, and their lives were closely intertwined for many years. Yet by the time Eric reached retirement, the two were living in different states and had not seen each other for a decade.

Then Ursula fell victim to Alzheimer's disease.

Eric faced the choice of arranging for Ursula to receive institutional care or caring for her himself. With the matter-of-fact manner of a man going out to shovel snow off a driveway, Eric packed up, leaving behind the solitude that he enjoyed, and moved in with Ursula.

I think Eric did not realize at the beginning how difficult caring for Ursula was going to be. On more than one occasion he said that if he had known, he would never have undertaken it. But this seemed an expression less of regret than of pain. For in the next breath he would say, "I just pray that God will help me take care of Ursula until the end."

Alzheimer's disease, which separates the victim from past and present, from others and from self, did not separate Eric and Ursula. Instead, the disease created the opportunity for a fearsome symmetry in their lives, creating a final period when Eric mothered Ursula as she long before had mothered him.

I am reasonably certain that Eric never thought about Naomi and Ruth as he urged Ursula to eat her vanilla wafers at lunch or helped her to the bathroom at night. But when I remember my uncle and aunt, I am reminded of Ruth's words to her mother-in-law: "Do not press me to leave you. . . . Where you go, I will go; where you lodge, I will lodge. . . . Where you die, I will die—there will I be buried" (1:16–17).

In the end, Ursula had to go into a nursing home. Soon after, Eric collapsed and died at home, while Ursula lived on another year. Today they are buried near each other.

A CHANCE MEETING

Questions to Begin

15 minutes
Use a question or two to get warmed up for the reading.

1 Describe a coincidence that has had a lasting impact on your life.

2 Think of times when you have been a stranger—marrying into a family, moving to a different city, starting a new job. Which of these experiences was the most difficult? What made it difficult? Who helped you get adjusted and accepted?

3 Describe a situation in which you were helped by an older person. What made this situation memorable? Describe a time when you helped someone much younger than you.

5 minutes
Read the passage aloud. Let individuals take turns reading
paragraphs.

The Reading: Ruth 2:1–23

Ruth Finds Unexpected Help

1 Now Naomi had a kinsman on her husband's side, a prominent rich
man, of the family of Elimelech, whose name was Boaz. 2 And Ruth
the Moabite said to Naomi, "Let me go to the field and glean among
the ears of grain, behind someone in whose sight I may find favor."
She said to her, "Go, my daughter." 3 So she went. She came and
gleaned in the field behind the reapers. As it happened, she came
to the part of the field belonging to Boaz, who was of the family
of Elimelech.

4 Just then Boaz came from Bethlehem. He said to the reapers,
"The LORD be with you." They answered, "The LORD bless you."
5 Then Boaz said to his servant who was in charge of the reapers,
"To whom does this young woman belong?" 6 The servant who was
in charge of the reapers answered, "She is the Moabite who came
back with Naomi from the country of Moab. 7 She said, 'Please, let
me glean and gather among the sheaves behind the reapers.' So she
came, and she has been on her feet from early this morning until now,
without resting even for a moment."

8 Then Boaz said to Ruth, "Now listen, my daughter, do not
go to glean in another field or leave this one, but keep close to my
young women. 9 Keep your eyes on the field that is being reaped, and
follow behind them. I have ordered the young men not to bother you.
If you get thirsty, go to the vessels and drink from what the young
men have drawn."

10 Then she fell prostrate, with her face to the ground, and
said to him, "Why have I found favor in your sight, that you should
take notice of me, when I am a foreigner?"

11 But Boaz answered her, "All that you have done for your
mother-in-law since the death of your husband has been fully told
me, and how you left your father and mother and your native land
and came to a people that you did not know before. 12 May the
LORD reward you for your deeds, and may you have a full reward
from the LORD, the God of Israel, under whose wings you have come
for refuge!"

13 Then she said, "May I continue to find favor in your sight, my lord, for you have comforted me and spoken kindly to your servant, even though I am not one of your servants."

14 At mealtime Boaz said to her, "Come here, and eat some of this bread, and dip your morsel in the sour wine." So she sat beside the reapers, and he heaped up for her some parched grain. She ate until she was satisfied, and she had some left over. 15 When she got up to glean, Boaz instructed his young men, "Let her glean even among the standing sheaves, and do not reproach her. . . ." 17 So she gleaned in the field until evening. Then she beat out what she had gleaned, and it was about an ephah of barley.

Naomi Perks Up

18 She picked it up and came into the town, and her mother-in-law saw how much she had gleaned. Then she took out and gave her what was left over after she herself had been satisfied. 19 Her mother-in-law said to her, "Where did you glean today? And where have you worked? Blessed be the man who took notice of you."

So she told her mother-in-law with whom she had worked, and said, "The name of the man with whom I worked today is Boaz."

20 Then Naomi said to her daughter-in-law, "Blessed be he by the LORD, whose kindness has not forsaken the living or the dead!" Naomi also said to her, "The man is a relative of ours, one of our nearest kin."

21 Then Ruth the Moabite said, "He even said to me, 'Stay close by my servants, until they have finished all my harvest.'" 22 Naomi said to Ruth, her daughter-in-law, "It is better, my daughter, that you go out with his young women, otherwise you might be bothered in another field."

23 So she stayed close to the young women of Boaz, gleaning until the end of the barley and wheat harvests; and she lived with her mother-in-law.

10 minutes
Choose questions according to your interest and time.

1 What sort of initial impression does Boaz make in 2:4?

2 Who serves whom in 2:14? How significant is this?

3 Ruth repeatedly speaks of finding favor (2:2, 10, 13). What does this say about her situation?

4 How is Naomi different at the end of chapter 2 from how she is in chapter 1? Who and what have caused the change?

5 Where can God's action be glimpsed in the events of this chapter?

A Guide to the Reading

If participants have not read this section already, read it aloud. Otherwise go on to "Questions for Application."

Background. Barley harvesting was labor for both men and women in the village. The men advanced through the field, cutting the stalks of grain a handful at a time and letting them fall to the ground. The women followed, gathering the stalks into bundles and then tying the bundles into sheaves.

Some grain inevitably escaped the harvesters, but they would not go back over the field to collect it. It was the custom to leave the stray stalks of grain for destitute people to pick up, or glean. In this way the community attempted to provide for its poorest members—people such as Naomi and Ruth.

2:1–3. Earlier the author made a point of mentioning Elimelech's clan (the Ephrathite clan—1:2). Now we hear that a well-off landowner named Boaz belongs to Elimelech's clan (2:1). When Ruth, without realizing it, chooses Boaz's field to glean in (2:3), we may be sure that something will come of it.

2:4–7. By midmorning the scene has been set. Ruth is gleaning in just the right place. The overseer has had a chance to form a favorable impression of her. At this very moment, Boaz appears (2:4). Can it be meaningless coincidence?

2:8–9. Boaz speaks kindly to Ruth. Notice that he calls her "my daughter" (2:8); he is of Naomi's generation. His speech, which in Hebrew is old-fashioned, characterizes him as a courteous older person—just the kind of person Ruth needs to meet.

2:10. Judging by Ruth's outpouring of gratitude (2:10), Boaz has done her a favor beyond what the gleaning rules oblige him to do. Because of uncertainty about the meaning of some of the Hebrew words, scholars disagree about the precise nature of the extra benefit. But apparently Boaz lets Ruth work in the portion of the field normally off limits to gleaners. He tells her to "keep close" to the women who are gathering and binding the grain (2:8). This puts her in a better position to collect grain than if she had to stay back and pick up only the stalks that the harvesters accidentally passed over.

Literally, Boaz tells Ruth to "stick with" his female workers (2:8). The same Hebrew word describes how Ruth "clung to" Naomi (1:14). By some mysterious providence, Ruth's generous faithfulness in need is beginning to come back to her. As Edward F. Campbell Jr. comments, "One magnanimous act gives impetus to another." Like Ruth, Boaz is beginning to emerge as a person of generous faithfulness in need. His kindness to Ruth has the quality of faithfulness because Ruth is, through marriage, a member of his clan. But he goes beyond what ordinary faithfulness requires—just as Ruth has done with Naomi.

In chapter 2. A number of details create a sense of Ruth's vulnerability:

✦ Ruth asks permission to glean in the field (2:7) even though gleaning was an accepted custom. It may be that the land-owners expected gleaners to get their permission, wishing to control the gleaners' location and timing. In any case, Ruth's request highlights her dependence on the goodwill of strangers.

✦ Boaz asks, "To whom does this young women belong?" (2:5). This does not mean he thought she was someone's slave. Boaz simply assumes that as either family member or servant she belongs to a household headed by a man. But, of course, this is exactly Ruth's problem: she does not belong to a male-headed household. She is a person with no security or protection.

✦ Boaz and Naomi keep referring to the possibility of the male harvesters bothering Ruth (2:9, 15, 22), subtly implying that she is in danger of what we might call sexual harassment in the workplace. Boaz's directions to the men not to yell at her or interfere with her gleaning and Naomi's advice to stick with the women remind us that Ruth is an unmarried woman, probably in her early twenties and reasonably attractive. She is a stranger with no male relative to look out for her.

2:17–23. When Ruth sets the result of her labor before Naomi—thirty to forty pounds of grain—the older woman shows signs of life. In the morning Naomi made hardly any response to Ruth's proposal to go gleaning, but in the evening, in the presence of so much grain, she becomes quite chatty.

Questions for Application

40 minutes
Choose questions according to your interest and time.

1 When have you realized that God was working in a hidden way through circumstances in your life? Can we detect God's activity beneath the events of our lives?

2 Boaz had something to offer Ruth. What resources or skills do you have to offer to people in need? How generously do you offer what you have?

3 Verse 11 led one commentator to remark on how fine it is to report others' good deeds, yet how often we fail to do so, and even spread criticism of others instead. Would you agree or disagree? What difference does it make when we broadcast other people's charitable actions and failings?

4 Who are the vulnerable people in your family, parish, or town? What provisions does your community make for them? What needs go unmet? How do you know? How can you find out? Whom can needy people rely on for help? How do you contribute to their security? What more could you—and your parish—do?

"The original questions people come up with often beat the best study guide."

Dan Williams, *Starting (& Ending) a Small Group*

Approach to Prayer

15 minutes
Use this approach—or create your own!

♦ Let someone in the group read aloud the following words from St. Catherine of Siena's *Dialogue,* in which she records words spoken to her by Christ:

I ask that you love me with the same love with which I love you. This indeed you cannot do, because I loved you without being loved. Therefore to me, in person, you cannot repay the love which I ask of you. So I have placed you in the midst of your neighbors, so that you may do to them that which you cannot do to me, that is to say, that you may love your neighbor freely, without expecting any return. And what you do to them I count as done to me.

Allow a few minutes for silent reflection. Then give participants an opportunity to pray brief prayers aloud for people who are suffering a loss or a serious need of some sort. The leader can sum up the prayers with a final prayer asking God to help each person in the group express care for those who have been mentioned. End by praying the Our Father together.

A Living Tradition

A Kindly and Proper Gentleman

This section is a supplement for individual reading.

Nicolaus Serarius, a German Jesuit, wrote on Ruth in the seventeenth century. Reflecting on Boaz's conversation with Ruth in chapter 2, Serarius offered these thoughts on Boaz as a man of kindliness and propriety:

"Boaz said to Ruth, 'Now listen, my daughter'" (2:8). Boaz calls her "daughter" partly because of his age, which is greater than hers, and partly because he is a courteous and pleasant man. For although it would have been friendly and pleasant enough if he called her "young woman," it is kinder and more pleasant to call her "daughter."

"Do not go to glean in another field" (2:8). When an opportunity for doing good presents itself, it is a characteristic of a kind person to be glad and not let the opportunity slip away. People who are hard and sour and niggardly are unhappy when needy people come to their door asking for help or a contribution. They send them away immediately to other people's doors—sometimes shouting an insult after them. Our Boaz is far different from this. In his eyes Ruth is good luck and happiness itself, and he instructs her to stay in his field, not to turn aside to another.

"Keep close to my young women" (2:8). It is more respectable for her to stick with the young women, with whom her modesty and chastity will be better protected than if she worked with the men —which shows that Boaz had considerable prudence, dignity, and morality. In addition, Boaz had generosity and kindness in view in this instruction. Usually there is more compassion among women, so it seemed realistic to expect that the young women would be more kindly to the young woman, especially when they noticed that their master was well disposed and friendly to her.

"I have ordered the young men not to bother you" (2:9). Boaz indicates that he is greatly concerned not only that the harvesters should place no obstacle in the way of Ruth's gleaning but also that her purity and modesty should not be damaged by any unwelcome touch or impudent gesture or word.

Ruth Makes a Proposal

Questions to Begin

15 minutes
Use a question or two to get warmed up for the reading.

1 Married participants: Describe how you and your spouse got engaged. Unmarried participants: Describe what you know about your parents' engagement.

2 Have there been any May-December marriages among your relatives or friends? How did they work out?

The Reading: Ruth 3:1–18

A Daring Plan

[1] Naomi her mother-in-law said to her, "My daughter, I need to seek some security for you, so that it may be well with you. [2] Now here is our kinsman Boaz, with whose young women you have been working. See, he is winnowing barley tonight at the threshing floor. [3] Now wash and anoint yourself, and put on your best clothes and go down to the threshing floor; but do not make yourself known to the man until he has finished eating and drinking. [4] When he lies down, observe the place where he lies; then, go and uncover his feet and lie down; and he will tell you what to do." [5] She said to her, "All that you tell me I will do."

Is Boaz Willing?

[6] So she went down to the threshing floor and did just as her mother-in-law had instructed her. [7] When Boaz had eaten and drunk, and he was in a contented mood, he went to lie down at the end of the heap of grain. Then she came stealthily and uncovered his feet, and lay down.

[8] At midnight the man was startled, and turned over, and there, lying at his feet, was a woman! [9] He said, "Who are you?" And she answered, "I am Ruth, your servant; spread your cloak over your servant, for you are next-of-kin." [10] He said, "May you be blessed by the LORD, my daughter; this last instance of your loyalty is better than the first; you have not gone after young men, whether poor or rich. [11] And now, my daughter, do not be afraid, I will do for you all that you ask, for all the assembly of my people know that you are a worthy woman. [12] But now, though it is true that I am a near kinsman, there is another kinsman more closely related than I. [13] Remain this night, and in the morning, if he will act as next-of-kin for you, good; let him do it. If he is not willing to act as next-of-kin for you, then, as the LORD lives, I will act as next-of-kin for you. Lie down until the morning."

Things Hang in the Balance

[14] So she lay at his feet until morning, but got up before one person could recognize another; for he said, "It must not be known that the

woman came to the threshing floor." 15 Then he said, "Bring the cloak you are wearing and hold it out." So she held it, and he measured out six measures of barley, and put it on her back; then he went into the city.

16 She came to her mother-in-law, who said, "How did things go with you, my daughter?" Then she told her all that the man had done for her, 17 saying, "He gave me these six measures of barley, for he said, 'Do not go back to your mother-in-law empty-handed.'" 18 She replied, "Wait, my daughter, until you learn how the matter turns out, for the man will not rest, but will settle the matter today."

10 minutes
Choose questions according to your interest and time.

1 Ruth tells Naomi she will follow her instructions (3:5). But compare 3:4 and 3:9. Does Ruth go beyond Naomi's instructions? What might be the significance of this?

2 In an ancient Near Eastern village, a substantial citizen like Boaz might feel uncomfortable marrying a penniless foreigner like Ruth. What counterbalances any reluctance Boaz might feel about marrying Ruth?

3 After reading the dialogue between Naomi and Ruth in the first three chapters, how would you describe the relationship between the two women?

4 Would it be fair to describe Naomi's approach to Boaz as manipulative? Why or why not?

5 Drawing on everything in the story so far, what picture of Ruth would you paint? In what ways is she a good example for other people?

A Guide to the Reading

If participants have not read this section already, read it aloud. Otherwise go on to "Questions for Application."

Background. Ancient listeners had the advantage of knowing how Israelite clans operated. For example, they knew that in each clan certain men bore a special responsibility to fellow members. Hebrew had a technical word for these designated kinsmen—translated variously as "nearest kin" (2:20), "near kinsman" (3:12), and "next-of-kin" (3:9, 13). Ancient Israelites also knew that when a married man died without a son, his brother was supposed to marry the widow in order to care for her and father an heir for his deceased brother (Deuteronomy 25:5–10). A designated kinsman, however, was not legally obliged to do this for a widow in his clan, although he might feel a moral responsibility to do so.

Boaz, a designated kinsman for Ruth, is not duty bound to marry her. As far as we can tell, the idea has not entered his head during the seven weeks of harvesting (are guys sometimes slow about this sort of thing?). But he has shown generous faithfulness in need, which leads Naomi to suspect he might be willing to go beyond what is required—if he were asked at the right moment, in the right way. At times God sets things up without our having any idea what is going on (Ruth just happened to glean in the field of Boaz); at other times God works through human shrewdness.

3:1–5. Naomi advises Ruth to propose to Boaz. The plan does not involve seduction, although it calls for stealth, courage, and trust in Boaz's goodwill. Naomi tells Ruth to wash and put on perfumed oil; nothing unusual here, since oil was normally used with bathing (roll-on deodorants were a thing of the future). The translation says Ruth is to put on her "best clothes" (3:3), but the Hebrew word is a term for ordinary outerwear. Ruth is not to make herself gorgeous, just presentable.

Harvesting was somewhat festive, and most likely other villagers shared Boaz's meal and also slept on the threshing floor. This may explain why Naomi lays emphasis on Ruth's noticing exactly where Boaz lies down. It would hardly do to uncover someone else!

3:8–11. Ruth speaks of marriage in symbolic terms: "Spread your cloak over your servant" (3:9). She literally asks

Boaz to spread the wings, or corners, of his cloak over her. This is a symbol of both marriage and protection. Boaz used the same image on the morning he met Ruth: "May you have a full reward from the LORD . . . under whose wings you have come for refuge!" (2:12). It turns out that Boaz is the one whose wings will provide refuge for Ruth. God will fulfill Boaz's prayer for Ruth through Boaz.

Boaz immediately welcomes Ruth's proposal of marriage. He is indeed willing to go beyond the duties of a designated kinsman. Why does he praise her proposal as an instance of loyalty? The reason, apparently, is that if Ruth had pursued marriage with a man her own age, the children born would have no relationship to Naomi. However, if Ruth marries Boaz, a designated kinsman, the first son will be considered an heir of Elimelech and Mahlon and will be, in a sense, Naomi's son. By proposing to Boaz, Ruth is again acting in Naomi's best interests.

3:12–13. But there is a wrinkle. Another designated kinsman has precedence over Boaz in caring for Elimelech's family. When it comes to marrying Ruth, he has the right of first refusal.

Do Boaz and Ruth have sex on the threshing floor? Because another clan member must be consulted, they are not yet free to marry, and in any case Israelite custom would not sanction their consummating their marriage agreement in that way. Nothing in the narrative says they do. When Boaz tells Ruth to "lie down until the morning" (3:13), he uses a Hebrew word without sexual connotations. It simply means "lodge for the night." Ruth used the same word when she told Naomi, "Where you lodge, I will lodge" (1:16). Ruth's words of faithfulness are again being echoed back to her. Yet the whole scene is obviously sexually suggestive. How much of Boaz does Ruth uncover? Significantly, in biblical Hebrew, the word *feet* can be a euphemism for the male genitals. There is a note of delight in Boaz's recognition of Ruth (3:10), and we have no reason to think that Ruth found Boaz undesirable. Presumably this faithful pair were virtuous at the threshing floor, but not without a certain effort!

3:15. Boaz sends a gift to Naomi. Ultimately the story is about Naomi's empty life—and how God filled it.

Questions for Application

40 minutes
Choose questions according to your interest and time.

1 What risks is Ruth taking by following Naomi's plan? When have you taken a risk for something you really wanted? What did you learn?

2 Both Boaz and Naomi give Ruth advice (2:8–9, 22; 3:1–4). How can you know when it is appropriate to give someone advice?

3 Who has given you wise advice? Whose advice do you trust? With whom do you discuss your relationship with God, your responsibilities, your decisions?

4 When has the welfare of a family member been an important consideration in a decision you have made regarding marriage, career, or place of residence? Do you face any such decision now?

5 Ruth trusts Naomi. Naomi trusts Boaz. How can you tell when a person is trustworthy?

"Our aim is to be *at home with* the Scriptures, not to become experts in scriptural exegesis."

James Rauner, *The Young Church in Action*

Approach to Prayer

15 minutes
Use this approach—or create your own!

✦ Use Ruth's risk taking as your point of departure. Let someone read aloud the following words by Cardinal Leo Josef Suenens, one of the leading figures at Vatican Council II:

There is an element of risk which you must preserve in your life, if you want it to be great and worthwhile. Make a brief examination of conscience on this point: 'Do I ever do anything which I would not have done if Christ had not come on earth?' If everything about you can be explained in human terms, then Christianity has not penetrated you to your very depths.

Will you take a risk in the name of Jesus? He is watching you; he is waiting for you. And he measures your heart's real love by the impulse which gets you out of yourself and makes you rebel against conformity. There is no need to be afraid of imitating St. Peter occasionally and walking on the water towards the Lord.

Allow a few minutes for silent reflection. Give the opportunity for brief, spontaneous prayers. End with the Our Father.

Saints in the Making

A Useful Balance

This section is a supplement for individual reading.

Ruth knew how to decline advice and how to receive it. She was certainly a woman with a mind of her own: her refusal in chapter 1 to leave Naomi shows that clearly enough. Yet Ruth was also willing to be guided by her mother-in-law, as we see in chapter 3. Ruth's balance of strong-minded determination and openness to guidance can be seen in the lives of many of the saints. For example, consider St. Philip Neri.

Philip was a priest in Rome during the sixteenth century. The Romans of the day, including many of the clergy, could hardly be described as wholehearted followers of Christ. For many of them, Christianity was a veneer; for some, it was even a vehicle for self-advancement. Philip cultivated friendships with people at every level in the city, from beggars to cardinals. He worked in informal ways, for example, strolling with friends through the quiet streets at siesta time and leading them to his apartment for a reading from the biography of a saint and a little prayer. Over a period of several decades he led so many people to a renewed relationship with Christ that he came to be called the Apostle of Rome.

Philip's casual methods stood in stark contrast to the almost military approach of St. Ignatius of Loyola, founder of the Jesuits, who lived in Rome at the same time. Philip admired Ignatius, but when Ignatius suggested that he join the early Jesuits, Philip declined. Philip knew that he was called to something quite different.

Once, however, after reading about missionaries, Philip got the idea of abandoning his outreach in Rome and traveling to the East Indies—modern Indonesia—to evangelize. But first he sought advice. Philip was forty; the man he consulted, a monk named Vincenzo Ghettini, was eighty. After a few days of prayer, Vincenzo gave Philip his advice: "Your Indies are in Rome."

Thus on one occasion Philip was clear minded enough to turn aside advice that would have led him away from the particular path he felt God had placed him on. But on another occasion his faithfulness to his calling was protected by his willingness to seek the advice of a holy older person.

Boaz Takes Care of Business

Questions to Begin

15 minutes
Use a question or two to get warmed up for the reading.

1 When have you undertaken a special responsibility to care for a member of your family?

2 When good things happen in your life, who celebrates with you?

Opening the Bible

5 minutes
Read the passage aloud. Let individuals take turns reading
paragraphs.

The Reading: Ruth 4:1–22

Legal Maneuvering

1 No sooner had Boaz gone up to the gate and sat down there than the next-of-kin, of whom Boaz had spoken, came passing by. So Boaz said, "Come over, friend; sit down here." And he went over and sat down. 2 Then Boaz took ten men of the elders of the city, and said, "Sit down here"; so they sat down.

3 He then said to the next-of-kin, "Naomi, who has come back from the country of Moab, is selling the parcel of land that belonged to our kinsman Elimelech. 4 So I thought I would tell you of it, and say: Buy it in the presence of those sitting here, and in the presence of the elders of my people. If you will redeem it, redeem it; but if you will not, tell me, so that I may know; for there is no one prior to you to redeem it, and I come after you." So he said, "I will redeem it."

5 Then Boaz said, "The day you acquire the field from the hand of Naomi, you are also acquiring Ruth the Moabite, the widow of the dead man, to maintain the dead man's name on his inheritance." 6 At this, the next-of-kin said, "I cannot redeem it for myself without damaging my own inheritance. Take my right of redemption yourself, for I cannot redeem it."

7 Now this was the custom in former times in Israel concerning redeeming and exchanging: to confirm a transaction, the one took off a sandal and gave it to the other; this was the manner of attesting in Israel. 8 So when the next-of-kin said to Boaz, "Acquire it for yourself," he took off his sandal.

9 Then Boaz said to the elders and all the people, "Today you are witnesses that I have acquired from the hand of Naomi all that belonged to Elimelech and all that belonged to Chilion and Mahlon. 10 I have also acquired Ruth the Moabite, the wife of Mahlon, to be my wife, to maintain the dead man's name on his inheritance, in order that the name of the dead may not be cut off from his kindred and from the gate of his native place; today you are witnesses."

11 Then all the people who were at the gate, along with the elders, said, "We are witnesses. May the LORD make the woman who is coming into your house like Rachel and Leah, who together built up the house of Israel. May you produce children in Ephrathah and

bestow a name in Bethlehem; 12 and, through the children that the
LORD will give you by this young woman, may your house be like
the house of Perez, whom Tamar bore to Judah."

A Child for Naomi—and the World

13 So Boaz took Ruth and she became his wife. When they came
together, the LORD made her conceive, and she bore a son. 14 Then
the women said to Naomi, "Blessed be the LORD, who has not left
you this day without next-of-kin; and may his name be renowned in
Israel! 15 He shall be to you a restorer of life and a nourisher of your
old age; for your daughter-in-law who loves you, who is more to you
than seven sons, has borne him." 16 Then Naomi took the child and
laid him in her bosom, and became his nurse. 17 The women of the
neighborhood gave him a name, saying, "A son has been born to
Naomi." They named him Obed; he became the father of Jesse, the
father of David.

18 Now these are the descendants of Perez: Perez became
the father of Hezron, 19 Hezron of Ram, Ram of Amminadab,
20 Amminadab of Nahshon, Nahshon of Salmon, 21 Salmon
of Boaz, Boaz of Obed, 22 Obed of Jesse, and Jesse of David.

10 minutes
Choose questions according to your interest and time.

1 How does the women's statement about Ruth in 4:15 compare with Naomi's attitude toward Ruth implied in 1:21?

2 What does 4:15–16 suggest about the relationship between Naomi and Ruth as the story ends?

3 Ten generations are identified in 4:18–22, the same number as the years of difficulty that Naomi experienced (1:1–5). What might be the significance of this correspondence?

4 Have the problems and questions raised in chapter 1 been solved or answered?

5 What does this reading tell us about what God is like?

A Guide to the Reading

*If participants have not read this section already, read it aloud.
Otherwise go on to "Questions for Application."*

Background. The scene shifts to the men's side of village
life: the sphere of business and legal affairs. Villages operated on
the basis of customary laws about family obligations and rights
of inheritance. Legal actions required an assembly of leading men
who knew the law and could act as notaries to transactions.

Business was conducted in the spacious area in front
of the city gate. Here Boaz gathers the other designated kinsman
and the men of the town (4:1–2).

The technicalities Boaz is dealing with are not entirely
clear, since the Hebrew terms translated "buy," "redeem," and
"acquire" are not fully understood. However, here is one possible
reconstruction. In ancient Israel, land was supposed to stay with
the clan. Consequently an individual owner was not free to sell
his land permanently and absolutely. If circumstances compelled
him, he could sell the use of his land. But then a member of the
clan had the right—and duty—to buy it back and restore it to
the family.

Elimelech had apparently owned property in Bethlehem.
When he left town, he probably sold the use of his land and took
the proceeds with him. Perhaps now Naomi holds the right to buy
back the use of her deceased husband's land. But being a woman
and impoverished, she cannot exercise her right. So she offers to
transfer the right to someone else in the clan (4:3).

4:3–4. Boaz asks the other designated kinsman whether
he wants to acquire the right to buy back the use of Elimelech's
land. If so, the kinsman will be authorized to approach the current
occupant of the land and negotiate a price for its return. Initially
the kinsman assents.

4:5–6. But then Boaz points out that along with the legal
right goes a moral responsibility. If the kinsman acquires the benefit of regaining Mahlon's land, it would be just and fair for him also
to assume responsibility for Mahlon's widow (4:5), even if he is
not, strictly speaking, obliged to do so. This puts the designated
kinsman in a bind. If he acquires the right to redeem Elimelech's
land, he has two options: (1) He can marry Ruth. But if they have
a son, the boy will be considered the son of Mahlon and thus the

heir of the property. When the boy grows up, the kinsman will have to hand over the land to him—and lose whatever he has paid to redeem it. (2) He can refuse to marry Ruth. But then he will look like a stingy fellow to the men of the town, whom Boaz has shrewdly assembled to witness the negotiations. The kinsman will be shamed for failing to do his utmost for his relatives.

The kinsman decides to lose neither money nor honor (4:6). He is like Orpah, to the extent that both are willing to do what is expected for a relative, but not more. Orpah showed affection, however, while the kinsman shows only calculation.

4:9–10. Boaz, like Ruth, is willing to go beyond the minimum in providing for those who have a claim on his care. He also shows himself to be like Naomi—clever in sizing up other people and bringing practical matters to a successful conclusion.

4:13–17. When last we catch sight of Ruth, she is being led by Boaz in a wedding procession to his house (4:13). We are pleased, if not surprised, to hear that she later gives birth to a boy. What is surprising is to hear the women proclaiming, "A son has been born to Naomi" (4:17). Yet their congratulations bring out the point of the story. Because Ruth has been so faithful as to marry a kinsman of Naomi's husband, Elimelech, the first son is considered Elimelech's heir and thus a child of hers. (By the way, the Hebrew word translated "nurse" in 4:16 means that Naomi cared for Obed, not nursed him at the breast.) Naomi now has a grandson to support her in old age. Through the loyalty of those around her, God has filled the empty Naomi with barley and a baby, with sustenance and security.

4:17–22. At the end the author places Naomi, Ruth, and Boaz in a larger picture. Boaz and Ruth become great-grandparents of David, the greatest king in the history of Israel. Through David, they will be ancestors of Jesus, the savior of the world (Matthew 1:1–17). In caring for Naomi, Ruth and Boaz have not been shortchanged. As scholar Katrina Larkin comments, "God uses the faithfulness of ordinary people to achieve great things."

Questions for Application

40 minutes
Choose questions according to your interest and time.

1 When has God seemed to empty your life and then fill it again in a new way? How has this affected your relationship with God?

2 Where are you less like Ruth and Boaz and more like Orpah and the other designated kinsman?

3 How is God calling you to imitate Ruth or Boaz?

4 When have you seen the impact a small act of kindness can make? What opportunities for small acts of kindness have you been neglecting?

5 Have you realized that you are part of a larger plan that God has been unfolding—a plan that affects other people? What have you learned from this?

Pauses in the discussion are not cause for discomfort. "Silent moments afford opportunities for letting God's message resonate and slowly deepen in each individual."

Loretta Girzaitis, *Guidebook for Bible Study*

Approach to Prayer

15 minutes
Use this approach—or create your own!

✦ The women of Bethlehem
acknowledged God as the
source of all life and blessings
(4:14–15). End by thanking
God for his goodness. Give
people a chance to mention
one or two things they are
especially thankful for. Then
pray either Psalm 65 or Psalm
92 together.

A Living Tradition

Final Thoughts on Ruth

This section is a supplement for individual reading.

Ancient Christian writers were struck by Ruth's significance as an ancestor of Jesus and as a foreigner who joined God's people, the Israelites. Here is a sample of their reflections:

The women who bring the baby Obed to Naomi say, "Blessed be the Lord, for this child will be a restorer of life for you" (4:14–15). According to their ordinary perception, the child was obviously going to bring pleasure to Naomi. In reality, he was going to bring conversion to the world, for from his line would eventually blossom forth Jesus, the savior of the world.

Theodoret, fifth-century bishop of Cyrrhus, in modern Syria

God has been pleased to raise up among human beings a new race in which people are no longer set into the opposites of slave and free, poor and rich, Jew and gentile. It is Christ who has brought about this glorious condition. In expectation of his coming, God carefully arranged everything in the old covenant as an image of Christ as copy to original, as shadow to body. Thus the wise God, wishing to offer a likeness of what was to come, used the entry into the Israelite nation of gentile women such as Ruth to give us a picture of the entry of the nations into Christ and the elimination of human divisions.

Isho`dad, ninth-century bishop of Hedatta, in modern Iraq

To all of us belonging to foreign peoples Ruth was established as the greatest example, so that doing the same things she did, we might gain from God the same benefits. It made sense, then, that as Matthew the evangelist was going to announce the good news of God's call and adoption of the foreign peoples, he placed Ruth in the genealogy, instructing us foreign peoples through her. By her example, the evangelist shows us that if we leave behind our native lands we too will be filled with the good things that follow, and we will not be counted as belonging to foreign peoples, but to the true Israel, the people of the inheritance of God.

Eusebius, fourth-century bishop of Caesarea, in modern Israel

An Uncomfortable Possibility

Not every religious tradition would find a place among its sacred writings for a story like Jonah's. Religious communities generally parade their saints but forget about the members who fall short of their ideals. Every group has an inclination to airbrush away the warts of its representative figures and portray them as larger than life.

The book of Jonah does not fit this pattern at all. Jonah is the story of a smaller-than-life prophet who was less responsive to God than the people he preached to. Preserving such a story was, for the Israelite people, an exercise in self-criticism—a way of saying, "Here's how we tend to go wrong."

Yet the story of Jonah is right at home in the Bible, for the Bible is a virtual library of self-criticism. In Genesis the people of Israel recorded the misdeeds of their ancestors: Jacob played his father for a fool, and his sons sold their brother Joseph into slavery. The Bible's historical books detail the failings of Israel's kings— from David, who murdered one of his officers and took his wife, to Ahab, who murdered a poor neighbor to get his land. The prophetic books are full of warnings that the people of Israel ignored. The Gospels are unanimous in reminding Christians that on the night Jesus was arrested, his preeminent follower denied knowing him. Page after page in Scripture recounts the failings of our ancestors in faith and by implication reminds us of our own shortcomings.

The story of Jonah reminds us that there is no automatic connection between belonging to God's people and being in tune with God. Jonah shows that it is possible in one sense to know God while in another sense to hardly know him at all—and suggests that religious people are peculiarly susceptible to confusing superficial knowledge of God with real knowledge.

The story brings out this message through a contrast between two different types of knowers. The author presents a prophet who seems to have a direct phone line to God and pagans who have only incomplete and erroneous ideas about God; in fact, they worship a variety of false gods. At every step, the prophet knows God and the pagans do not—or is it the other way around?

When the storm hits, the sailors say, "Let us cast lots, so that we may know on whose account this calamity has come upon us" (1:7). They have no idea what God is up to, but they are determined to find out. When the lot falls to Jonah, he tells them, "I know it is because of me that this great storm has come upon you" (1:12). Jonah is well informed about God's plans; he just doesn't like them.

The Ninevites are vague about God. With their limited theological background they cannot be sure there is any way of being reconciled to him. The most they can say is, "Who knows? God may relent and change his mind; he may turn from his fierce anger" (3:9). In any case, they are willing to repent. In contrast, Jonah has no doubts about what God is like: "That is why I fled to Tarshish at the beginning; for I knew that you are a gracious God and merciful, slow to anger, and abounding in steadfast love, and ready to relent from punishing" (4:2). Jonah's knowledge of God stands out starkly as the very reason for his resistance to God! In one sense, Jonah knows God quite accurately; in a deeper sense, not at all.

The author of Jonah invites us to reflect on an uncomfortable possibility. Are we like Jonah—able to give perfect catechism answers to religious questions (see 1:9; 4:2) and pray in the finest manner (see 2:2–9), but not deeply knowing the God of love? Have we been possessed and transformed by this God, whose mercy goes out to every man and woman around us?

God saw the objections to his love that lay hidden in Jonah's heart beneath the surface of his piety. God sent Jonah on a mission that brought the conflict into the open (4:2). This gave Jonah the opportunity to turn from his narrowheartedness and embrace the mercy of God toward other people (4:10–11). Perhaps God will send each of us on missions of service that will reveal our resistance to his love—so that we might be healed.

Would You Believe It?

A young woman was troubled with doubts about God. She went occasionally to talk with a priest about them. One day the priest missed their appointment, and while the woman waited at the parish office, she got into a conversation with the janitor.

A seemingly trivial encounter. Yet more than thirty years later, it has turned out to be life changing.

In the course of their conversation, the janitor told the young woman how Jesus had been reshaping his life. The woman was intrigued. Later the janitor introduced her to some Christian friends, and through their witness she found a renewed faith in God. Not only that, but she and one of the friends got married, and they had six children.

Looking back, we can see that the woman was in the right place at the right time. Yet at the time she had no inkling of the effect her chance meeting would have on her—and through her, on many other people.

There is an incident of this sort in the story of Ruth. One morning Ruth goes to glean in the barley fields around Bethlehem without knowing which residents own the various fields. "As it happened," she picks the field of Boaz (2:3). The Hebrew, more literally "it happened by happenstance," emphasizes that she has no idea of the significance of her choice.

By midmorning Ruth has made a favorable impression on the foreman of the harvesters with her politeness and hard work. At this point the author uses a little word to make the story vivid. Our translation renders it, "Just then Boaz came from Bethlehem" (2:4). At that very moment—wouldn't you know it?—Boaz shows up. In the right place, at the right moment, just the right thing happened. The storyteller can't help being amazed by the coincidence.

Ruth and Boaz have a conversation that has long-range consequences not only for them but also for many other people. Boaz and Ruth are deeply impressed with each other at their meeting in the barley field. Within a couple of months they have become husband and wife. Through their first son they become ancestors of David, the greatest king of Israel—and, through David, ancestors of Jesus.

What if Ruth had chosen a different field to glean in? What if Boaz had stayed in town that day? Things could easily have happened differently. As it turned out, things fell into place. Without realizing it, Ruth chose the right field. Without any awareness of the destiny he was about to discover, at just the right moment—lo and behold!—Boaz arrived on the scene.

The author of Ruth says little about God's action. The characters acknowledge God as the source of blessings (1:6; 2:4; 4:11–12, 14), but the story shows us God's action rather than speaking about it. Furthermore, God's action in the story is neither obvious nor miraculous. God works through the mysterious growth of crops and children. He works through the generous faithfulness of Ruth and Boaz. He works in a hidden way to arrange the circumstances of people's lives. Only at rare moments, as when Ruth and Boaz happen to meet in the field, do we catch a glimpse of the Weaver's hand interlacing the threads of human lives.

This is how most of us usually experience God's action: hidden for the most part, but sometimes detectable by hindsight as we see how he has arranged things. God's action may seem especially visible in the seemingly chance encounters that have turned out to be decisive for us, those times when everything seemed to have been perfectly arranged, when—would you believe it?—just the right thing happened.

It is comforting to reflect on such coincidences, for they help us trust that God is always weaving the fabric of our lives, even when we see only the threads.

This line of reflection is also humbling. It reminds us that God chooses to weave dark threads among the bright ones (it was widowhood that brought Ruth and Boaz together), and who can understand why? It leads us to consider how much the course of our lives depends on chance meetings—on events, that is to say, that are utterly beyond our control. The lo-and-behold moments remind us to what a great extent our happiness ultimately depends not on us but on the divine Weaver.

Suggestions for Bible Discussion Groups

Like a camping trip, a Bible discussion group works best if you agree on what you're undertaking together, why you're doing it, where you hope to get to, and how you intend to get there. Many groups use their first meeting to reach a consensus on such questions. Here is a checklist of issues, with a few bits of advice from people with experience in Bible discussions. (A planning discussion will go more smoothly if the leaders have thought through the following issues beforehand.)

Agree on your purpose. Are you getting together to gain wisdom and direction for your life? to finally get acquainted with the Bible? to support one another in following Christ? to encourage those who are exploring—or reexploring—the Church? for other reasons?

Agree on attitudes. For example: "We're all beginners here." "We're here to help each other understand and respond to God's Word." "We're not here to offer counseling or direction to each other." "We want to read Scripture prayerfully." What do *you* wish to emphasize? Make it explicit!

Agree on ground rules. Barbara J. Fleischer, in her useful book *Facilitating for Growth,* recommends that a group clearly state its approach to the following:

+ Preparation. Do we agree to read the material before each meeting?

+ Attendance. What kind of priority will we give to our meetings?

+ Self-revelation. Are we willing to help the others in the group gradually get to know us—our weaknesses as well as our strengths, our needs as well as our gifts?

+ Listening. Will we commit ourselves to listen to each other?

+ Confidentiality. Will we keep everything that is shared with the group in the group?

+ Encouragement and support. Will we give as well as receive?

✦ Participation. Will we work to allow everyone time and opportunity to make a contribution?

You could probably take a pen and draw a circle around *listening* and *confidentiality*. Those two points are especially important.

The following items could be added to Fleischer's list:

✦ Relationship with parish. Is our group part of the religious education program? independent but operating with the express approval of the pastor? not a parish-based group at all?

✦ New members. In the course of the six meetings, will new members be allowed?

Agree on housekeeping.

✦ When will we meet?

✦ How often will we meet? Meeting weekly or every other week is best if you can manage it. William Riley remarks, "Meetings once a month are too distant from each other for the threads of the last session not to be lost" *(The Bible Study Group: An Owner's Manual).*

✦ How long will meetings run?

✦ Where will we meet?

✦ Is any setup needed? Christine Dodd writes that "the problem with meeting in a place like a church hall is that it can be very soul-destroying" given the cold, impersonal feel of many church facilities. If you have to meet in a church facility, Dodd recommends doing something to make the area homey *(Making Scripture Work).*

✦ Who will host the meetings? Leaders and hosts are not necessarily identical.

✦ Will we have refreshments? Who will provide them?

✦ What about child care? Most experienced leaders of Bible discussion groups discourage bringing infants or other children to adult Bible discussions.

Agree on leadership. You need someone to facilitate—to keep the discussion on track, to see that everyone has a chance to speak, to help the group stay on schedule. Rena Duff, editor of the newsletter *Sharing God's Word Today,* recommends having two or three people take turns leading the discussions.

It's okay if the leader is not an expert regarding the Bible. You have this booklet, and if questions come up that no one can answer, you can delegate a participant to do a little research between meetings. It's important for the leader to set an example of listening, to draw out the quieter members (and occasionally restrain the more vocal ones), to move the group on when it gets stuck, to remind the members of their agreements, and to summarize what the group is accomplishing.

Bible discussion is an opportunity to experience the fulfillment of Jesus' promise "Where two or three are gathered in my name, I am there among them" (Matthew 18:20). Put your discussion group in Jesus' hands. Pray for the guidance of the Spirit. And have a great time exploring God's Word together!

Suggestions for Individuals

Y ou can use this booklet just as well for individual study as for group discussion. While discussing the Bible with other people can be a rich experience, there are advantages to individual reading. For example:

✦ You can focus on the points that interest you most.

✦ You can go at your own pace.

✦ You can be completely relaxed and unashamedly honest in your answers to all the questions, since you don't have to share them with anyone else!

My suggestions for using this booklet on your own are these:

✦ Don't skip "Questions to Begin." The questions can help you as an individual reader warm up to the topic of the reading.

✦ Take your time on "Questions for Careful Reading" and "Questions for Application." While a group will probably not have enough time to work on all the questions, you can allow yourself the time to consider all of them if you are using the booklet by yourself.

✦ Since you are going through Jonah and Ruth at your own pace, consider doing some additional reading also.

✦ You might find it helpful to make notes on your reflections, either in the pages of this booklet or in a separate notebook or journal. This is a way of holding on to your insights into Jonah and Ruth and recording your thoughts about what these stories mean for you.

✦ Give yourself plenty of opportunities to reflect on the meaning of Jonah and Ruth for you. Let your reading be an opportunity for the words of these stories to become God's words to you.

Resources

Bibles

The following editions of the Bible contain the full set of biblical books recognized by the Catholic Church, along with a great deal of useful explanatory material:

+ The Catholic Study Bible (Oxford University Press), which uses the text of the New American Bible

+ The Catholic Bible: Personal Study Edition (Oxford University Press), which also uses the text of the New American Bible

+ The New Jerusalem Bible, the regular (not the reader's) edition (Doubleday)

Books

+ Edward F. Campbell Jr., *Ruth*, The Anchor Bible (Garden City, N.Y.: Doubleday, 1975).

+ James Limburg, *Jonah: A Commentary*, The Old Testament Library (Louisville, Ky.: Westminster John Knox Press, 1993).

+ Kirsten Nielsen, *Ruth: A Commentary*, The Old Testament Library (Louisville, Ky.: Westminster John Knox Press, 1997).

+ Jack M. Sasson, *Jonah*, The Anchor Bible (New York: Doubleday, 1990).

How has Scripture had an impact on your life? Was this booklet helpful to you in your study of the Bible? Please send comments, suggestions, and personal experiences to Kevin Perrotta c/o Trade Editorial Department, Loyola Press, 3441 N. Ashland Ave., Chicago, IL 60657.